MAY 1 5

Tell Me Why

WHY?

Giraffes Have Long Necks

Katie Marsico

Published in the United States of America by Cherry Lake Publishing
Ann Arbor, Michigan
www.cherrylakepublishing.com

Content Adviser: Dr. Stephen S. Ditchkoff, Professor of Wildlife Sciences, Auburn University, Auburn, Alabama
Reading Adviser: Marla Conn, ReadAbility, Inc.

Photo Credits: © PathDoc/Shutterstock Images, cover, 1, 15; © xavier gallego morell/Shutterstock Images, cover, 1, 11; © michaeljung/Shutterstock Images, cover, 1, 5, back cover; © sevenke/Shutterstock Images, cover, 1, 13; © J Reineke/Shutterstock Images, cover, 1; © Janvdb95/Shutterstock Images, cover, 1, 19; © Anna Omelchenko/Shutterstock Images, 5; © MattiaATH/Shutterstock Images, 7; © EBFoto/Shutterstock Images, 9; © EcoPrint/Shutterstock Images, 11; © Pyty/Shutterstock Images, 15; © Stacey Ann Alberts/ Shutterstock Images, 17

Library of Congress Cataloging-in-Publication Data

Marsico, Katie, 1980- author.
  Giraffes have long necks / by Katie Marsico.
    pages cm. -- (Tell me why)
  Summary: "Offers answers to their most compelling questions about this long-necked animal that uses its height to reach leaves at the very top of trees. Age-appropriate explanations and appealing photos. Additional text features help students locate information and learn new words."-- Provided by publisher.
  Audience: K to grade 3.
  Includes bibliographical references and index.
  ISBN 978-1-63188-003-2 (hardcover) -- ISBN 978-1-63188-046-9 (pbk.) -- ISBN 978-1-63188-089-6 (pdf) -- ISBN 978-1-63188-132-9 (ebook) 1. Giraffe--Juvenile literature. 2. Children's questions and answers. I. Title. II. Title: Tell me--why do giraffes have long necks?

  QL737.U56M38 2015
  599.638--dc23
                    2014005727

Cherry Lake Publishing would like to acknowledge the work of The Partnership for 21st Century Skills.
Please visit www.21stcenturyskills.org for more information.

Printed in the United States of America
Corporate Graphics Inc.
July 2014

Table of Contents

Reaching Toward the Treetops

Heads up! Anna shades her eyes from the sun. She glances toward a clump of trees in one of the zoo **habitats**. Suddenly, she sees two large, gentle eyes staring back at her. They belong to a giraffe!

Anna is amazed by how far the animal's neck stretches. It reminds her of a **crane** reaching high above the ground. Her neck doesn't look like that! So why do giraffes have such a long neck?

LOOK!

What do you see the giraffes in this picture doing? What do you notice about their necks? How about the rest of their bodies?

A giraffe's long neck is one of its most unique physical features.

5

Giraffes are the tallest land animals on Earth. They tower 14 to 18 feet (4.3 to 5.5 meters) above the ground. This means they would be able to peek inside the upper windows of a two-story house!

Yet there aren't too many houses where giraffes live. In the wild, they are mainly found in Africa's flat, grassy plains. Giraffes are herbivores. An herbivore is an animal that only eats leaves and other plant matter.

Giraffes find their food on the plains of Africa.

Giraffes are mammals. A mammal is a **warm-blooded** animal that is usually covered in hair or fur. Female mammals are able to produce milk to feed their babies.

Giraffes live in groups called herds. Most herds are made up of 12 to 15 animals. Being part of a group offers giraffes protection from their main enemy—lions. A giraffe's ability to run fast and kick hard also helps it survive.

A baby giraffe drinks its mother's milk.

No Ordinary Neck

Anna tilts her own neck back to gaze up at the giraffe. Moving her neck allows her to move her head. A giraffe uses its neck to do the same thing.

Yet Anna's neck doesn't make up one-third of her total height. A giraffe's neck does. It stretches up to 6 feet (1.8 m) high! It weighs about 600 pounds (272 kilograms). That's more than 10 times what Anna's whole body weighs!

MAKE A GUESS!

Giraffes must move their long neck backward and forward when they run. Why do you think that is?

A giraffe's long neck is used to move its head when running.

Surprisingly, people and giraffes have the exact same number of vertebrae in their necks. Vertebrae are the bones that join together to form the spine, or backbone. Each of a giraffe's seven neck vertebrae measures up to 10 inches (25 centimeters) in length.

This giraffe uses its long neck to reach a clump of leaves.

For Feeding or Fighting

Anna notices the giraffe nibbling leaves off one of the tall trees nearby. The zookeeper says giraffes eat plant matter that is 6 to 17 feet (1.8 to 5.2 m) above the ground. Some scientists think giraffes once had to **compete** with other animals to feed on lower-lying plants. It's possible that giraffes **adapted** by developing a longer neck. Then they were able to reach a separate food source: taller plants and trees.

ASK QUESTIONS!

What is the giraffe in this picture eating? Hint: A giraffe's diet is made up of leaves, shoots, buds, vines, flowers, and fruit.

Only a giraffe is able to reach food on the highest branches.

15

Other scientists say giraffes developed a longer neck not for feeding, but for fighting. Males often swing their necks at each other like clubs. Whichever giraffe proves stronger becomes the dominant, or more powerful, animal. This makes it easier to find **mates**.

Giraffes also use their long neck as a lookout tool. They are able to raise their head high above Africa's grassy plains. This allows giraffes to spot **predators**.

*Giraffes rely on their necks to view what is
happening around them.*

More About an Amazing Animal

Before Anna leaves, she watches the giraffe take a drink. It **splays** its front legs and bends its knees to reach a small pool of water. Anna thinks this doesn't look easy!

The zookeeper says there's a downside to having a long neck. Giraffes must stretch into a difficult position to drink. This makes them more **vulnerable** to predators hunting for their next meal.

Taking a drink is a difficult and sometimes dangerous activity for giraffes.

Anna decides she has a lot more to learn about giraffes. The zookeeper tells her to come back and visit again. She also surprises Anna by handing her a bucket filled with leaves. The zookeeper invites her to feed the giraffe.

Anna holds up a leaf and waits. The giraffe stretches over the fence. Thanks to its long neck, Anna enjoys an unforgettable experience with her new favorite zoo animal!

Some zoos allow visitors to feed giraffes.

Think About It

Humans and giraffes are vertebrates. This means they have backbones with vertebrae. What name describes animals without a backbone? See if you can list at least three examples of such animals.

Look carefully at the photographs you see in this book. Do you think that a giraffe's coloring helps it hide from predators in the wild? Why or why not?

Glossary

adapted (uh-DAHP-tuhd) changed to fit the needs of a new situation or environment

compete (kuhm-PEET) to try to get something that is also desired by others

crane (KRAYNE) a large machine with a long arm that is used to lift and move heavy objects

habitats (HA-buh-tatz) the places where plants and animals normally live and grow

mates (MAYTZ) animals that come together to reproduce

predators (PRED-uh-turz) animals that hunt and eat other animals

splays (SPLAYZ) moves legs or other limbs so that they spread open and apart from each other

vulnerable (VUL-nur-uh-buhl) open to attack or danger

warm-blooded (WARM-BLUH-duhd) having a body temperature that doesn't change because of outside temperature changes

Find Out More

Books:

Hanson, Anders. *Giraffes*. Minneapolis: ABDO Publishing Company, 2014.

Raatma, Lucia. *Giraffes*. New York: Children's Press, 2013.

Riggs, Kate. *Giraffes*. Mankato, MN: Creative Paperbacks, 2013.

Web Sites:

National Geographic Kids—Giraffes
www.kids.nationalgeographic.com/kids/animals/creaturefeature/giraffe
Visit this Web page for additional information about giraffes, including photos, a video, and an e-card.

San Diego Zoo Kids—Giraffe
www.kids.sandiegozoo.org/animals/mammals/giraffe
Check out this Web site for photos of giraffes, as well as more fun facts about them.

Index

About the Author

Katie Marsico is the author of more than 150 children's books. She lives in a suburb of Chicago, Illinois, with her husband and children.